South West Coast Path:
South Cornwall Coast

Land's End to Plymouth

Part of the England Coast Path

Northern Eye

First published in 2019, reprinted in 2024 by:

Northern Eye Books Limited
Northern Eye Books, Tattenhall, Cheshire CH3 9PX

© Northern Eye Books Limited 2019-2023

ISBN 978-1-908632-71-5

Text: Dennis and Jan Kelsall

Series editor: Tony Bowerman

Photographs: Dennis and Jan Kelsall, Tony Bowerman, Adobe Stock, Alamy, Dreamstime, Shutterstock

Design: Carl Rogers and Laura Hodgkinson

Dennis and Jan Kelsall have asserted their rights under the Copyright, Designs and Patents Act, 1988 to be identified as the authors of this work. All rights reserved.

A CIP catalogue record for this book is available from the British Library.

Printed in the EU by Latitude on woodland-friendly FSC stock

Cover: *St Michael's Mount (Walk 2)*

www.northerneyebooks.co.uk
www.englandcoastpath.co.uk

@northerneyebooks
@england_coast_path

@northerneyeboo

@northerneyebooks

For sales enquiries, please call 01928 723 744
tony@northerneyebooks.co.uk

Important Advice: The routes described in this book are undertaken at the reader's own risk. Walkers should take into account their level of fitness, wear suitable footwear and clothing, and carry food and water. It is also advisable to take the relevant OS map with you in case you get lost and leave the area covered by our maps.

Whilst every care has been taken to ensure the accuracy of the route directions, the publishers cannot accept responsibility for errors or omissions, or for changes in the details given. Nor can the publisher and copyright owners accept responsibility for any consequences arising from the use of this book.

If you find any inaccuracies in either the text or maps, please write or email us at the address above. Thank you.

This book contains mapping data licensed from the Ordnance Survey with the permission of the Controller of Her Majesty's Stationery Office. © Crown copyright 2023 All rights reserved. License number 100047867.

Contents

South West Coast Path 4
Top 10 Walks: South Cornwall's Coast 6

1 | Land's End 8
2 | Perranuthnoe 14
3 | The Loe 20
4 | Lizard Point 24
5 | Helford Estuary 30
6 | St Anthony Head 36
7 | Nare Head 40
8 | Dodman Point 46
9 | Polruan & Lantic Bay 52
10 | Rame Head 58

Useful Information 64

South West Coast Path

Running for 630 miles from Minehead in Somerset, around the tip of Land's End and back to South Haven Point at the mouth of Poole Harbour in Dorset, the South West South West Coast Path is Britain's longest National Trail. Bordered by the Bristol and English channels and looking out to the open Atlantic, it encompasses some of England's most spectacular and wildest coastline, where the diversity of plant, animal and insect life can be stunning. The seas, coves and surrounding hinterland has been a dramatic setting for a gloriously rich history, which have inspired countless tales of romance, drama and intrigue.

This series of Top Ten Walks explores highlights along the way; showcasing its natural beauty, wildlife and heritage and provoking imagination. Who knows, you may be inspired to come back to tackle the complete trail.

St Michael's Mount is a fortified tidal island in Mounts Bay, South Cornwall

South Cornwall's Coast

From Land's End at the western tip of England to Penlee Point at the entrance to Plymouth Sound, Cornwall's convoluted south coast is infinitely varied, ranging from rugged cliffs battered by the full force of the Atlantic to the sheltered Cornish Riviera where the weather, scenery and flora can be almost Mediterranean. Snaking inlets, creeks and river estuaries take the unceasing creep and fall of the tide deep into the heartland, while on the coast, an endless succession of fine strands and sheltered coves compete with the best beaches in the world. Cornwall may be a popular summer destination, but there are any number of corners where you can walk the cliffs, hardly seeing a soul all day.

"This little peninsula called Land's End, in which there lies an immense treasure and many things worth notice…"

Daniel Defoe *A tour Through the Whole Island of Great Britain*

TOP 10 Walks: South Cornwall's Coast

FOR MANY, THE ICONIC, EXTREMITY DESTINATIONS of Land's End and Lizard Point are a must and the views from the cliff edge are simply awe-inspiring. But there is so much more to this coast and these ten walks explore its many facets, from the highest cliffs to tiny coves of rock pools, soft sand and crystal sea, and secluded tidal creeks to Cornwall's unusual largest lake, kept apart from the sea by only a narrow bank of shingle. Keep your eyes peeled and you will see many birds, perhaps the rare chough or a peregrine falcon, while out to sea you might spot seals, dolphins or even a whale.

Land's End — page 8

Perranuthnoe — page 14

The Loe — page 20

Lizard Point — page 24

The setting sun reflected through the Enys Dodnan rock arch

walk 1

Land's End

An impressive walk around the western-most tip of mainland England

What to expect:
A steep lane at the start, but otherwise undulating field and coast paths

Distance/Time: 8.5 kilometres/ 5¼ miles. Allow 3 to 3½ hours

Start: Sennen Cove Harbour car park (pay and display)

Grid ref: SW 350 263

Ordnance Survey map: Explorer 102 *Land's End*

Refreshment: Choice of pubs and cafés at both Sennen Cove and Land's End

Walk Outline

After climbing a lane from the pretty harbour of Sennen Cove to the village, the route winds past old Coastguard cottages, across fields and along a lane to Trevescan. There's more field walking past Trevilley before turning down to the coast at Nanjizal. The route then follows the Coast Path to Greeb Farm, bypassing the Land's End theme park on its seaward side. The way continues past Maen Castle to the lookout on Pedn-mên-du before dropping back to the harbour.

Land's End

In Cornish, *Pedn-an-Laaz*, Land's End is the most westerly point of mainland England and has been an iconic destination for travellers since the 17th century. Daniel Defoe visited in 1724, but it was the arrival of the railway at Penzance in 1852 that truly put it on the tourist map. Horse-drawn carriage excursions were laid on for day-trippers, with refreshment and gifts hawked to visitors. Although not everyone is excited by the modern tourist theme park or the crowds it attracts, the coastal scenery remains as stunning as ever and you can't deny a certain thrill in standing at the 'end of the land'.

Fingerpost at Land's End

Chough

The Walk

1. Follow the street back from the **car park**, turning right at the corner and then keeping left up **Stone Chair Lane**. At the top, go right. Reaching the end, opposite **Longships Watch holiday cottages**, turn left past houses and continue along a drive towards a row of former **Coastguard cottages**.

2. Approaching **gates**, branch right through a **kissing gate** and carry on beside the left wall. Keep the same direction in the next couple of fields then bear right across a final rough pasture to emerge on a drive by **Treve Moor House**. Follow it out to the main road.

3. Cross to the road opposite and carry on to **Trevescan**. Turn off right along a drive almost opposite the road junction and walk past a **couple of cottages** to find a path leaving over a stile in the left corner. Head away by the right hedge bank, but then cross to continue on its opposite side. Halfway along, look for an **ancient cross** standing on the other side of the wall. Leaving the field, pass through the **farmyard at Trevilley** and cross a stile by the **phone box library** onto a track.

4. Go right and immediately left, but as the tarmac then turns into another yard, keep ahead on a grass track.

© Crown copyright and/or database right. All rights reserved. Licence number 100047867

Aerial view of the First and Last House at Land's End

Carry on in a second field until the hedge curves right, there bearing diagonally across to a gap in the far corner. Continue with the hedge on your left, shortly passing into the adjacent field at a shallow corner. Strike across to find a narrow hedge gap at the far side. A contained path swings right (ignore the path then off left), the bordering hedges soon giving way to bracken as it approaches the coast. Steadily steepening, a dramatic view opens of the cliffs, coves and tiny beach below.

5. Meeting the **Coast Path**, go right above **Nanjizal** for the spectacular finale to the walk. Sheer cliffs, zawns and stacks all vie for attention, particularly impressive being **Enys Dodnan**, a stack pierced by a tall arch through which the sea surges.

Eventually reaching **Greeb Farm**, keep with the higher path, shortly branching off left to pass around the seaward side of the **Land's End theme park**. Carry on to the **First and Last House**, which stands on the most westerly finger of the peninsula.

Dr Syntax was the hugely popular

Looking out towards the Longships Lighthouse from Land's End granite cliffs

early 19th-century satirical creation of caricaturist Thomas Rowlandson and writer William Combe, a bumbling, pompous village curate who wandered the countryside in search of the then fashionable 'Picturesque' landscape. The tip of the headland is said to resemble the character's pointed, jutting chin.

The tradition of 'end to end' walking might be said to have begun in 1871, when the brothers John and R Naylor, prosperous Warrington timber merchants, walked from John o' Groat's to Land's End in exactly two months, observing Sundays as days of rest. Their meandering course took in many places of interest and clocked up 1,372 miles. It became popularised as a challenge after Dr Barbara Moore's much publicised hike in 1960 (23 days) and a road walking race, organised later the same year by Billy Butlin. The shortest road distance is around 830 miles, while a typical off-road route linking National Trails is around 1,200 miles and takes 56 days or more.

6. Having gazed upon the cliffs below and the view to the **Longships and the lighthouse**, leave along the **Coast Path**, heading northeast towards **Sennen**.

Further along is a small headland, **Maen Castle.** *The site of an Iron Age promontory fort, it is protected on its landward side by a substantial stone wall.*

Continue above the cliffs to a **castellated building**. *It was built in 1912 as a Coastguard lookout.*

7. The ongoing **Coast Path** descends across the steep slope to the **village**.

Follow the street ahead to find the **harbour car park** on your right to complete the walk. ♦

Sennen Cove
Gone are the days when pilchards were caught in such numbers that they had to be shovelled onto the quayside; yet a handful of boats still sail from the harbour, returning mainly with crab and lobster. Just 25 miles to the west are the Isles of Scilly, visible from the headland on a clear day. Closer to, sunk beneath the waves lies the legendary land of Lyonesse, the fabled site of King Arthur's final battle.

St Michael's Mount seen from the South West Coast Path near Perranuthnoe

walk 2

Perranuthnoe

An undemanding yet enjoyable walk that looks out to St Michael's Mount, one of Cornwall's most famous sights

What to expect:
Undulating coast and field paths

Distance/Time: 8.5 kilometres/ 5¼ miles. Allow 2½ to 3 hours

Start: Perranuthnoe car park (pay and display)

Grid ref: SW 539 294

Ordnance Survey map: Explorer 102 *Land's End*

Refreshment: The Victoria Inn, Perranuthnoe | 01736 710309 | www.victoriainn-penzance.co.uk OR Peppercorn Café, Perranuthnoe | 01736 719584 | www.thepeppercorncafe.weebly.com

Walk Outline
Starting from the village car park above Perran Sands, the walk immediately takes to the coast, heading west around Maen-du Point to Basore Point. The route then turns inland back to Perranuthnoe and continues across hillside fields past Trevean and Acton Castle to Prussia Cove. Once more on the coast, there is a delightful return past Cudden Point and above shallow coves to Perran Sands.

Perranuthnoe
The earliest evidence of occupation in the area is in an old field name suggesting a Neolithic tomb, and tin is known to have been mined since the Bronze Age. However, it wasn't until the mid-18th century that the industry developed. For over a century tin, copper and silver were produced, generating high profits. But the mainstay of life here was farming; barley, oats, turnips and potatoes were the chief crops with seaweed used as a fertiliser on the fields. Fishing too from small boats was important, the coastal waters yielding abundant catches of mackerel and pilchard.

Thatched shed, Prussia Cove

Freshly-caught mackerel

A standing stone overlooking Cudden Point, near Perranuthnoe

The Walk

1. Leave the **car park** left towards the sandy beach, but then immediately turn right over a stile with the **Coast Path**. A sandy track follows the field edge atop low cliffs above a rocky shore, soon rounding a point to bring St Michael's Mount into view. Carry on, later passing steps down to the shore and sweeping by a **viewpoint**. The path then diverges from the coast. Keep left for the views as it splits either side of a hedge, before long, rising to a crossing track.

2. Follow the track right, which, as you approach **Perranuthnoe**, develops as a lane. Passing below **St Pyrin and St Michael's Church**, turn off right down a side lane. Keep with it, curving right and then left to a junction opposite the **Peppercorn Café**.

3. Although the car park is just down to the right, the walk continues left up the hill to a staggered crossroad (The **Victoria Inn** is just down to the left). Turn off right along a drive beside **Churchway Cottage** to find a small gate on the right by a couple of wooden garages. Walk on at the edge of successive fields, in time

Walk 2 – Perranuthnoe

rising to a fork in the path. Stick with the left branch which, before long, leads to into a **yard**. Walk through to the end of a lane.

4. Cross to a track opposite between buildings into a field and carry on by the left hedge. Over a stile in the corner, go right and then left around the perimeter of the next field to **Trevean Farm**. Ignore a path off right past **Beare's Den Campsite** and instead keep ahead through a yard, joining a track that leads out to a lane.

5. Turn right along a **private road**. A short distance along, a stile on the left begins a parallel path in the adjacent field, but if overgrown, carry on a little further to pick it up through a gate into the next field along. Continue beside the hedge into a third field, at the far end of which, swing within the corner past **Acton Castle** (glimpsed through the hedge). Over a stile at the top of the field, bear right across the next field to an indented corner and walk on with the hedge on your right to emerge onto a lane.

6. Go right. At the end, swing right towards the entrance of a **car park**.

St Michael's Mount silhouetted against the setting sun across Mounts Bay

However, just before it, turn left along a private drive. Walk beside the car park to meet the **Coast Path** above Prussia Cove.

Prussia Cove gets its name from the late 18th century smuggler John Carter, who tenanted the cliff-top farm and styled himself King of Prussia. Despite his staunch Methodism, he and his brothers operated a lucrative 'free trade' business, regularly sailing to the French coast to return with tea, brandy and other luxuries for which there was a healthy local demand. His landlord was John Stackhouse, a gentleman biologist who owned Acton Castle, and it is said, though never proven, that tunnels run from its cellars to caves backing the coves below.

7. Take the right branch. Approaching the gate to a **thatched cottage**, bear left and continue past a path off left a few metres further on that leads down to the **cove**. Before long, the path rises past an **old fisherman's hut**; note the small brick structure opposite, a boiler for cooking the shellfish catch. A short distance beyond, branch left with the **Coast Path**, soon passing the remains of a rocket post strategically sited on the headland. Carry on along the coast, passing another rocket post before rising onto the neck of **Cudden Point**.

8. Cresting the ridge, the view opens across the bay to St Michael's Mount before the path descends steeply to run above lower cliffs. Eventually, beyond **Trevean Cove**, the path splits either side of a hedge; that on the left allows the better view. Later at a junction, go right to meet a track and turn left. Angling away from the coast, it leads to a junction by a house.

9. Go left and then keep left along a lane towards **Perranuthnoe**. At the end, turn right back to the **car park** to complete the walk. ♦

St Michael's Mount

Isolated at high tide, St Michael's Mount offered a secluded site for early monasticism, and a monastery existed there from the 8th century until the Dissolution. For a while, it belonged to the Benedictine house of its namesake in Normandy. During the 17th century, the island village flourished as a seaport but declined after the harbour at Penzance was developed following the arrival of the railway. Its picturesque setting makes it one of Cornwall's iconic views.

A shingle bar holds back the waters of The Loe, Cornwall's largest natural lake

walk 3

The Loe

An easy walk around the The Loe, Cornwall's largest natural lake

What to expect:
Good tracks and woodland paths, a short stretch along shingle bank

Distance/Time: 11 kilometres/ 6¾ miles. Allow 3 to 3½ hours

Start: Penrose Hill National Trust car park (donations)

Grid ref: SW 639 258

Ordnance Survey map: Explorer 103 *The Lizard*

Refreshment: The Stables Café (NT), Penrose | 01326 561407 | www.nautibutice.co.uk

Walk Outline
Leaving the lower end of the car park, join a winding track through the Penrose estate before following the bank of The Loe north towards the Cober valley. Swinging across the marshland at the head of the lake, the way traces its eastern shore to the coast. Join the Coast Path across the shingle of Loe Bar before climbing away to head back above the western bank. The way leads past the Penrose Stables Café and Walled Garden before returning on the outward track to the car park.

The Loe
Originally the valley of the River Cober, The Loe was flooded by rising sea levels at the end of the last Ice Age. The shingle bar, sealing it from the sea, was created by longshore drift, in which wind and wave action continually moves pebbles along the coast. The lake is an important site for overwintering birds and the area is rich in plantlife and home to several rare species including certain pondweeds and strapwort, the latter reintroduced in 2015. The lake is one of two, the other being on Bodmin moor, into which Sir Bedivere is said to have cast King Arthur's legendary sword, *Excalibur*.

Overlooking Loe Bar

Kingfisher

The Walk

1. From the bottom of the **car park** by an **information panel,** drop to a drive and follow it right. At a junction, swing sharp left and then at the next junction go right again. Reaching a third junction, turn left and carry on to cross a **stone bridge**.

2. Keep going as another track joins, the lake now in view ahead. Approaching the water, the drive swings left past a lodge and on through **woodland**. After 800 metres, take a path off right, which passes into **carr** and over a **bridge** spanning the **River Cober**. Rising beyond to another track, turn right.

3. At a later fork, keep right on a gravel track, passing through trees to run beside meadow. The way soon closes with the water, its reedy banks glimpsed through the trees. Keep right at another fork, after which, steps lead to a vantage looking out across the water to the Penrose lodge and stables. At the junction there, keep right with the footpath, shortly reaching another **viewpoint** beneath a stand of gnarled pine, which looks ahead to the shingle bar. Drop back into **Degibna Wood** to a junction, the path right merely leading to the shore. The other rises to a crossing path, which you should follow to the right, forking right again a little further on.

4. Joining with a **bridleway** and soon breaking into open grass, **Loe Bar** appears not far ahead. However, you're not there yet, for the path first winds around **Carminowe Creek**. Reaching a **farm track**, bear right to **Lower**

© Crown copyright and/or database right. All rights reserved. Licence number 100047867

Woodland carpeted in spring bluebells on the Penrose estate

Pentire. Again keep right and carry on past the head of the water to a junction.

5. Turn right over a **bridge**, a **walkway** continuing across marsh to a path on the opposite bank. Follow it beside the lake to the **coast** and **shingle bar**.

6. Again, the onward way is to the right, climbing off the far end of the bar along a track. At the top, a track doubles back past **Bar Lodge** and continues above the lake. Ignore paths off left, eventually rising over a low hill and reaching a signed junction near **Penrose**. Keep ahead to pass the **Stables Café**, the track then looping back to meet your outward route at Point (**2**). Head left back to the **car park** to complete the walk. ♦

The Penrose estate

The Penrose estate had been held by only two families since the 13th century, until The Loe and surrounding lands and coast were gifted to the National Trust in 1975. Although the house remains private, there is free access along many woodland and lakeside paths and within the stables is an excellent café. The walled gardens are being restored and are open to visitors, and there is a varied programme of events throughout the year.

Low tide exposes acres of golden sand at Kynance Cove

walk 4

Lizard Point

A superb walk taking in the southernmost point of mainland Britain

What to expect:
Undulating coastal path with some steeper sections, good inland paths and some lane

Distance/Time: 13.5 kilometres/ 8½ miles. Allow 2½ to 3 hours

Start: Lizard Point National Trust car park (pay and display)

Grid ref: SW 702 116

Ordnance Survey map: Explorer 103 *The Lizard*

Refreshment: Wavecrest, Lizard Point | 01326 290898 | www.wavecrestcornwall.co.uk OR Polpeor Café, Lizard Point | 01326 290939

Walk Outline
The walk immediately takes to the coast, heading from Lizard Point to Kynance Cove where there is a good path to the beach. The way continues over the open heath of Lizard Downs. Over the main road, it crosses rough grazing to a lane. There follows a stretch of tarmac walking before turning off across the fields past a small church. Winding on, the route regains the coast above Cadgwith and follows the cliffs all the way back to the car park at Lizard Point.

Lizard Point Lighthouse
The English Channel is the busiest shipping lane in the world with over 500 ships passing through every day. Receiving the full brunt of Atlantic weather and with a treacherous coastline and offshore reefs, the area has always represented a hazard to passing vessels. The first ligh, installed in 1619, lasted barely ten years. One hundred and twenty years passed before a second light was established, the twin towers originally holding open fires. Subsequently taken over by Trinity House in 1771, they have been upgraded over the centuries. The station was automated in 1998, while the Heritage Centre opened in 2009.

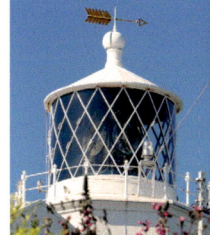
Lizard Point Lighthouse

Bottlenose dolphins

The Walk

1. Head down past **toilets** towards the coast, winding left and right to meet the **South West Coast Path**. Follow it right onto **Lizard Point**. *In the cove below is the point's first lifeboat station, which was established in 1859.* Head back up the track past a small **car park** before turning off left with the **Coast Path** in front of the **Wavecrest Café**. Carry on above the cliffs, winding around tiny coves and, down to the beach. The onward route, however, is up to the right, swinging left before the car park to meet a broader track.

2. To the left, the track dips across the head of a **small valley.** Rising beyond, watch for a path forking off right onto the **heath**. It soon leads to a crossing path, where you should turn right again. Head out across the open heath of

© Crown copyright and/or database right. All rights reserved. Licence number 100047867

Lizard Point Lighthouse at dusk

Lizard Downs towards distant houses, which soon appear ahead.

Sweeping behind the cliffs, the vast swathe of the **Lizard National Nature Reserve** *heath has colour throughout the year. Gorse, heather (four different types including the Cornish heath), squill, sea campion and thrift provide a backdrop, but there are many rarities too. In sheltered folds, look for cushions of bright yellow hairy greenweed, thyme broomrape, green-winged orchid and cat's ear. Surprisingly, there are 14 species of clover, of which twin- and long- headed grow only here in Britain.*

The Lizard orchid, whose delicate, pinkish flower indeed resembles its namesake, attracts pollinating flies with a subtle scent of goat. A very special, but threatened habitat lies in the centuries old rutted trackways that cross the down, which create sheltered, seasonal pools where three-lobed water-crowsfoot, pygmy rush and camomile can be found

At the far side, through a gate, walk on between trees to meet the main road.

3. Cross to a track opposite, which leads through a yard and then between wide-spaced hedges. A path continues

Visitors throng to the Lizard, Britain's most southerly mainland point

beyond its end to emerge onto a lane. Go right, later keeping ahead past a bend at **Chyheira Farm** onto a narrower lane for another 300 metres.

4. Watch for a track leaving back left through a gate to **St Grada Church** and carry on at the field edge. Ignoring the stile in the corner, turn within the field, passing a gate to find another stile in the next corner. Continue along a hedged path and then a grass swathe past sapling trees to emerge onto a junction of lanes at **Prazegooth**.

5. Go left and bear right with the minor lane past a cottage. Keep right where it splits and subsequently swing around a sharp left bend. The track ultimately leads down to **Cadgwith**, but the route takes a path off right to meet the **Coast Path**.

6. Follow it right, passing an awesome collapsed cave known as the **Devil's Frying Pan**, the sea surging in through a massive opening far below. The way undulates on above impressive cliffs for the next 2 kilometres before meeting a concrete track by **Church Cove**. Go left and right to resume the path, which leads on to Lizard Point's operational **lifeboat station** in **Kilcobben Cove**, relocated there in 1961. Past the top building the **Coast Path** continues around **Hot Point** to **Bass Point**, skirting below a **National Coastwatch station**.

7. Walking on, glance back to see the **castellated white building** of a former Lloyd's Signal Station, while a little further on, **two wooden huts** housed the Lizard Wireless Station. Beyond the **Housel Bay Hotel**, the path drops to **Housel Cove**, climbing steeply beyond for a final easy stretch past the **Lizard Lighthouse** before turning up past the **Youth Hostel** to the **car park** to complete the walk. ♦

Lizard Point lifeboat

The first Lizard lifeboat was established on the cliffs above Polpeor Cove following the wreck of the Czar off Bass Point in 1859. The Coastguard managed to save some crew, but the captain and his family perished. Since then, boats have operated from Cadgwith, Church Cove and Kilcobben Cove, where the present station was rebuilt in 2012 to house a new Tamar class vessel, named the Rose.

A tranquil summer scene on the Helford Estuary

walk 5

Helford Estuary

Fascinating creeks are explored on this leisurely ramble beside the Helford River estuary

What to expect:
Undulating riverside and field paths, short stretches along quiet lanes

Distance/Time: 11 kilometres/ 7 miles. Allow 3¼ to 3¾ hours
Start: Helford car park (pay and display)
Grid ref: SW 759 261
Ordnance Survey map: Explorer 103 *The Lizard*
Refreshment: The Shipwrights Arms, Helford | 01326 231235 | www.shipwrightshelford.co.uk, Holy Mackerel Café, Helford | 01326 231008 OR The New Inn, Manaccan | 01362 231301 | www.thenewinnmanaccan.co.uk

Walk Outline
Beginning from a car park above the village, the walk traces the wooded banks of the estuary towards the sea, passing delightful coves before climbing onto the promontory of Dennis Head. Dropping to St Anthony-in-Meneage, it returns beside Gillan Creek. Leaving the water, the route heads inland past Manaccan, and then across fields and through woodland to the head of Frenchman's Creek. Heading back there is another secluded cove and rocky Helford Point before returning past the village pub to the car park.

Helford River
Like many of the estuaries winding far back into the Cornish heartland, the Helford River is a *ria* or drowned river valley, created when sea levels rose after the last Ice Age. The villages around its banks developed as busy ports exporting granite and farm produce while bringing in coal and other local supplies. Although a few fishing boats remain, today's sea-going traffic is largely pleasure craft. Nevertheless, the passenger ferry to Helford Passage remains a vital link, particularly for Coast Path walkers, who would otherwise face a very long detour.

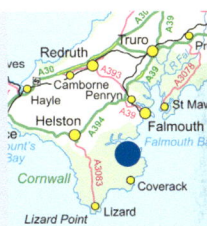

Helford Ferry

Little egrets

The Walk

1. Leaving the **car park** entrance, cross left to join the **South West Coast Path**, which parallels the lane within a belt of trees. Emerging onto the lane, turn uphill to a sharp bend, there taking the track ahead signed to 'St Anthony'. An undulating path continues through trees beside the **broadening estuary**, later dropping past the secluded heads of **Bosahan Cove** and **Ponsence Cove**. Eventually leaving the woods, the onward path is contained beside fields to a kissing gate and three-way sign.

2. Bear left on the loop out to **Dennis Head**, keeping left again at a later fork. The path encircles the gorse-covered headland that separates Gillan Creek from the main Helford estuary, ultimately returning you to the three-way sign at Point (**2**). Now bear left, dropping across an open field to a gate, from which a track leads out to a lane by **St Anthony's Church**. After calling in at the 14th-century church, which has a fine barrel roof and is lit only by candles, walk down to **Gillan Harbour**.

3. Head away along the lane above the creek. Ignore the path off across stepping stones to Gillan, but you can take a later concessionary path, which dips through the **shore woodland** and is an alternative to the tarmac. Returning

© Crown copyright and/or database right. All rights reserved. Licence number 100047867

Little egrets feeding in Gillan Creek at low tide

to the lane, walk a little further to find a gated track, signed as a footpath, which leaves sharp right off the bend.

4. Climb away, later breaking from the trees and winding by **cottages** to meet another track. To the right it leads to **Manaccan**, coming out opposite its **church**.

5. There's a **pub** here; you'll find it by going left and left again at a cross roads. However, the onward route is to the right, meeting the main lane by **South Café**. Go right and then first left along **Minster Meadow**. Keep left where it splits, but then immediately go right alongside the first house. Walk on at the field edge to come out onto another lane.

6. Cross diagonally left to a hedge-gap and continue straight across the field. Swinging left beside trees at the far side, the path shortly drops within the

The Helford Estuary seen from the rocks below Helford village

woodland fringe crossing occasional stiles. Ignore a later crossing path and keep left at the subsequent fork, eventually meeting a field track. Follow it to the right, winding out onto a lane at **Kestle Barton**.

7. Take the gated track opposite. At the bottom, where it bends left, go right beside **Frenchman's Creek**. After 800 metres, at a junction, turn up right, later forking left with the creek-side path. Approaching a private gate, go right, shortly emerging onto a drive. Turn right, keeping right again at a later junction towards 'Helford'.

8. Leaving the top of the field, take the first track off on the left, again signed towards 'Helford'. Where it later forks, branch down right to reach **Penarvon Cove**. Go right at the head of the beach to find the **Coast Path**, which winds around the cove and then out past cottages to a track. Follow it down to the bottom, where a track off left leads to the ferry. The **jetty head** provides a good **viewpoint** across the river.

9. Return and continue past the **Shipwrights Arms** through the **village**, coming alongside its creek. The **footbridge** beside the **ford** was washed away during a storm in March 2018, so until it is ever repaired, continue a little further to loop around the head of the creek on the road bridge. Return downstream and carry on uphill back to the **car park**, where an old chapel now serves as the **Holy Mackerel Café**, to complete the walk. ♦

Frenchman's Creek

The author Daphne du Maurier spent most of her life in Cornwall, which served as a setting for many of her books. 'Frenchman's Creek' is a tale of 17th-century adventure and love between Dona, bored both with her husband and court life, and a French pirate, who is using their disused country house as a secret base. Walking beside the creek today, it is not hard to imagine the setting as a place for their clandestine meetings.

Bird's-eye view of St Anthony Head and its lighthouse

walk 6

St Anthony Head

An almost wholly coastal walk exploring the beautiful Roseland peninsula at the mouth of Falmouth estuary

What to expect: *Occasional steeper climbs on coastal paths and quiet lane*

Distance/Time: 10.5 kilometres/ 6½ miles. Allow 3½ to 4 hours

Start: Porth Farm National Trust car park (pay and display)

Grid ref: SW 867 329

Ordnance Survey map: Explorer 105 *Falmouth & Mevagissey*

Refreshment: The Thirstea Co, Porth Farm | 01872 581898 | www.thethirsteacompany.co.uk

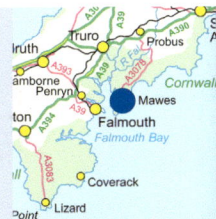

Walk outline
The route drops to Porth Creek and follows its wooded bank around North-hill Point and on to Place House. Back on lane, it winds behind the sheltered cove and past the church before regaining the coast and the onward path to St Anthony Head. After exploring the headland and military defences, the way continues along the cliff path beneath Drake's Downs and back around the Killigerran headand to Towan Beach. There is access to the shore before returning to the car park.

St Anthony Head
St Anthony Head marks the tip of the Roseland peninsula and, with Pendennis Point, stands guard over the estuary mouth, where Falmouth's deepwater docks shelter merchant and naval ships. They were once the base for the Falmouth Packet Service, which provided a mail service to the Empire for 160 years. Henry VIII fortified Pendennis with a castle in 1540, while on this shore a late 19th-century battery provided coastal defence through two World Wars. Now restored by the National Trust, there is much to see including the gun emplacements, magazines and lookout post.

Lighthouse, St Anthony Head

Peregrine

The Walk

1. Leaving the main, surfaced **car park**, go left and left again in front of a **cottage**. Bear right across a **grass car park**, picking up a wooded path from its far corner, which runs beside a lane. Over a **bridge**, swing right, the path soon curving at the foot of a meadow above the shoreline of **Porth Creek**. Returning to woodland, continue around **Northhill Point**. Remain with the lower path, eventually passing a path off to the ferry landing stage.

2. Meeting a lane, go left passing an expansive lawn fronting **Place House**. After some 300 metres leave right along a waymarked track. It leads past **St Anthony's Church**, a historic building cared for by the Churches Conservation Trust. Carry on, the way signed to 'St Anthony Head', turning right and then left to be beside the water again. A little further on, leave through a gate on the left and climb the field edge. Through a gate at the top is a view across the estuary to St Mawes Castle.

A trod slants down to continue above the shore before rising around **Carricknath Point**. With St Anthony's lighthouse now in view, the path dips behind **Molunan beach** and climbs to a junction beyond.

3. Go right, shortly passing a small **white building**, which was the lighthouse paraffin store. The route then swings off sharp left with the **Coast Path**, but you might first walk down to the **lighthouse** itself. It is not open to the public but there is a view from the gate. Climb back

© Crown copyright and/or database right. All rights reserved. Licence number 100047867

View to St Mawes Castle from St Anthony's Head

and go right with the **Coast Path** to find a path off right towards the top. It runs beneath the bastion walls to a **wartime observation station** and then to a **bird hide** beyond. Return to the **Coast Path** and climb to another junction. Fork right up shallow steps onto a drive by a **car park** and go right again, passing the former officers' quarters to reach the **magazines** and **gun emplacements**.

4. The **Coast Path** leads past the gun emplacements to undulate at the edge of **Drake's Downs**. There's a steep descent before the path climbs above **Porthbeor Beach**. Carry on around **Killigerran Head**. The way falls to a path coming up from the beach. Follow it inland, where a **courtyard** hosts **The Thirstea Co van**, and out to the lane opposite the car park, to complete the walk. ♦

St Anthony's Church, Place

The manor was once held by the Augustinian Priory at Plympton who established the church at Place around the 12th century. It is unusual in retaining its original medieval cruciform plan and has a finely carved Norman doorway brought from the priory. The central steeple is open to the church below, revealing its timber frame construction and solitary bell held high. The church also contains memorials to the Spry family of Place House.

Small boats crowd the slipway in Portloe harbour

walk 7

Nare Head

Strenuous ups and downs, but with two of Cornwall's prettiest villages and magnificent clifftop scenery

What to expect:
Steep climbs, field and clifftop paths, some quiet lanes

Distance/Time: 11 kilometres/ 7 miles. Allow 4 to 4½ hours

Start: Portloe car park (pay and display)

Grid ref: SW 938 396

Ordnance Survey map: Explorer 105 *Falmouth & Mevagissey*

Refreshment: The Ship Inn, Portloe | 01872 501356| www.staustellbrewery.co.uk OR New Inn, Veryan | 01872 501362 | www.newinn-veryan.co.uk

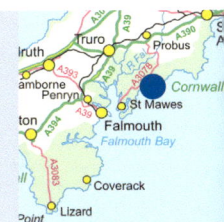

Walk Outline
Leaving the village of Portloe, the route climbs inland across the fields to nearby Veryan. Beyond, it falls along a steep sided valley to the coast at Carne Beach. Joining the Coast Path, it then follows the cliffs to Nare Head, the last stage climbing steeply from Tregagle's Hole. The way continues around the spectacular coast, with another descent and climb behind Kiberick Cove. Descending to Jacka Point, there is a fine view of Portloe before dropping to the harbour and the car park.

Nare Head
Although little remains visible today, Nare Head, together with its namesake 11 miles to the north east were strategic elements in the Second World War defence of Falmouth's dockyards. Nearly 240 such 'Starfish' sites were built to lure enemy bombers from their real objectives, displaying stray lights and fires to give the impression they had found their target. The site was requisitioned again during the Cold War, this time by the Royal Observer Corps with the construction of an underground bunker in 1962. It was intended to house three officers to monitor radioactive fallout after a nuclear attack.

Nare Head shelter

Pearl-bordered fritillary

emerge onto the main lane opposite **Jago Cottage**.

2. Turn left and then first right, continuing at the end of the drive on a grass track into a field. Keep straight ahead to a belt of trees, passing through to another field beyond. Bear left down to an indented corner of more trees and carry on a little further by the left fence to find a stile hidden in the trees. Over a stream, follow a path right emerging past a kiddies' **play area**. Either head straight out to the street or go left into the **churchyard** to have a look at **St Symphorian's Church**.

3. Walk out to the main street in front of the church and go left. Keep ahead past **The New Inn** and continue up the hill towards Pendower, passing between

The Walk

1. Leaving the **car park**, turn downhill to **Porthloe village**. Keep ahead above the **harbour** and climb past **The Ship Inn**. Some 200 metres further on, at a sign to 'Veryan', branch off right over a **bridge** on a drive to houses. Swing left to find a path leaving through a gate at the end. A trod heads uphill to a stile at the top. Cross and go left, leaving the field along a track to **Trewartha Hall Farm**. Through the yard, go right, the track then bending left. Carry on past a small settlement to

Summer wildflowers on the coast near Nare Head

two curious round, thatched houses. Beyond **Churchtown Farm**, leave over a stile on the left signed to 'Carne'. Stride away at the field edge to the far corner. *As you come out onto the lane, glance through the left hedge to see the overgrown mound of **Carne Beacon**, a Bronze Age burial and later beacon site. One of the largest in Britain, it is held to be the resting place of Saint Geraint, a 6th-century king of Cornwall. Legend tells that he was interred within the gold-plated boat which transported his body across the bay from his palace, but when the tomb was excavated in the 19th century, only a stone cist and ashes were found.*

4. Go right for 100 metres before abandoning the lane through a field gate on the left. Head away beside the hedge to a kissing gate in the next corner. The gorse covered mound then ahead is marked on the map as **Veryan Castle**, a defended Iron Age settlement. Turn half left, passing around gorse and slanting down to the base of the deep valley. Exit through a gate at the foot and walk out through a **car park** to the lane behind **Carne Beach**.

Portloe is a picturesque fishing village in a sheltered cove near Falmouth

5. Turn left to a bend and leave with the **South West Coast Path** up steps to the right. Head away above the cliffs, later dipping at the head of a small **cove** overlooked by a 19th-century ruin, **Mallet's Cottage**. *Although his wife lived in Veryan, Mallet spent much of his time here, where he moored his boat in the cove. In 1840, he abandoned his lot here for a new life in Australia, leaving his wife behind.*

The natural arch of Tregagle's Hole is a reputed haunt of the ghostly Jan Tregeagle, an unscrupulous 17th-century lawyer, who eventually sold his soul in greed to the devil and is condemned to wander and perform impossible tasks until Judgement Day.

It is then a steep climb above **Shannick Point**, where a path detours onto **Nare Head**.

6. Return to the main path and follow it on around the coast. Just offshore is **Gull Rock**, its inaccessibility making it an ideal breeding ground for a variety of seabirds. Further along, to the left is the grass-covered mound of a **Second World War bunker**. Nearby, low concrete structures are access and ventilation shafts of an **underground nuclear bunker**.

7. Beyond, there are several ups and downs, the path at one point carried on **duckboards** over springs seeping from the ground. Eventually, **Portloe** comes into view ahead, the old village squeezed into a narrow valley behind the cliff. A path off right takes you around **Jacka Point** before dropping to the **harbour**.

Climb to a junction in front of a **chapel** and turn right back up to the **car park**, to complete the walk. ♦

Veryan

The round, thatched houses at the edge of the village are two of five, built around 1820 by the Reverend Trist, reputedly for his daughters. They stand at the entrances to the village and, without corners, gave the devil no place to hide. Each carries a cross on its roof to further proclaim their sanctity. A local philanthropist, he also established separate schools for boys and girls and added a clock tower to the church

Sunset on Hemmick Beach, below Penare

walk 8

Dodman Point

A grand walk over the highest point on Cornwall's southern coast

What to expect:
Steep climbs, but good paths and tracks, short sections on quiet lanes

Distance/Time: 8 kilometres/ 5 miles. Allow 3 to 3½ hours

Start: Gorran Haven car park (charge)

Grid ref: SX 010 415

Ordnance Survey map: Explorer 105 *Falmouth & Mevagissey*

Refreshment: Choice of cafés in Gorran Haven

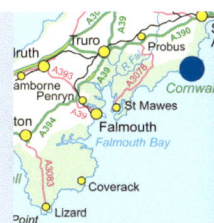

Walk Outline
Beginning in Gorran Haven, the route rises across hillside meadows by way of Treveague Farm to Penare. It is then steeply downhill to the coast at Hemmick Beach before immediately climbing to the cliffs. The way then undulates to Dodman Point, the highest point on Cornwall's south coast. There is easy walking around the peninsula followed by a long, gentle descent behind Bow Beach, to which there is access. A final pull onto Pen-a-maen brings Gorran Haven into view, the path dropping to the village behind the harbour.

Dodman Point
At 114 metres above sea level, Dodman or Deadman is the highest point along the southern Cornish coast. The Point owes its name, so legend says, to a terrible giant that once lived here. Having overeaten the village's livestock and children, the giant suffered a terrible stomach ache. The clever local doctor persuaded the giant that he needed bleeding. Soon the giant lay by the cliff, with blood coursing from his veins. And when the giant eventually weakened, the doctor simply tipped him over the edge into the sea. Predictably, there was great rejoicing when the doctor returned to the village.

'Fun Day', Gorran Haven

Ox-eye daisies

The Walk

1. Leaving the **village car park** turn right up the street. Keep right at a junction and carry on for a further 300 metres to a right-hand bend. Bear off left on a track, marked as a footpath, which leads up past houses to a gate into a **small wood**. Crossing a **stream**, carry on up the side of the valley, later winding past **cottages** to meet a lane at **Treveague Farm**.

2. Go briefly right before turning left at a sign to 'Penare' into a **camp site**. Fork left with the main track across the site and carry on beyond along a hedged path, which leads out to a junction of lanes.

3. Take the lane ahead to **Penare**, winding through with the main lane to pass the entrance to a **National Trust car park**. Just after, watch for a path leaving up **steps** on the left. Follow it right above the lane down to the coast at **Hemmick Beach**. If you're not going to the beach, you can save some climbing by cutting left across the top of the final field to join the **South West Coast Path**.

4. The route rises steeply onto the **cliffs**, later crossing seeping **springs** before winding up again. Easing off, the way continues to a gate at the **Bulwark**, a 600 metre-long Iron Age double rampart across the neck of the peninsula.

Looking back to Hemmick Beach from the Coast Path near Dodman's Point

The presence of Stone Age hunter-gatherers in the area is indicated by the discovery of microliths, tiny worked flints used to create barbs, points and teeth for spears and other tools. Permanent settlement came with the introduction of agriculture and the promontory enclosure at Dodman is one of the largest in Cornwall, possibly dating to a period some 200 years before the arrival of the Romans in Britain. Commonly termed 'forts', many played a defensive role but most were also villages with huts, work spaces, cultivation plots and livestock enclosures behind the stockade. The headland had in fact been occupied since the Bronze Age, as evidenced by two round barrows, and continued in use throughout the medieval period under strip field cultivation.

Carry on to the tip of **Dodman Point**, marked by a massive **granite cross**.

A disaster that should never have occurred was the loss of the MV Darlwyne in July 1966. An ex-Naval picket converted for pleasure cruising, it disappeared while returning from Fowey to Mylor. Despite the boat being unlicensed, ill equipped and in poor condition, and a warning of deteriorating weather that afternoon, the

The sheltered beach and harbour wall at Gorran Haven

captain left harbour with 29 passengers and his engineer. The alarm was eventually raised when the boat did not reach Mylor that evening and a full-scale search was launched at daybreak. Only twelve bodies were recovered and wreckage, assumed to be from the boat, was eventually discovered 50 years later by a diver off Dodman Point.

5. The **Coast Path** continues on around the point, eventually re-crossing the eastern end of the defensive earthwork. Keep going, the path shortly losing height behind **Bow Beach**, to which there is access at the far end.

6. Carry on around the point at **Pen-a-maen**, a final pull to be accomplished before dropping past the **Coast Path Café** to **Gorran Haven village** behind the beach.

Now a quiet backwater, Gorran Haven was a bustling fishing village in the 13th century, and recorded as being the first place in Cornwall where seine fishing was practised to catch pilchards. Still widely used across the world, the technique uses a long, weighted drift net hanging from floats like a curtain, which is laid out in an arc before the ends are brought together to entrap the fish. In a purse seine, a bottom draw line can also be pulled in to prevent the fish escaping from below. Such nets are particularly effective in catching fish that school together near the surface. Gorran's importance eventually declined during the 19th century, despite the construction of a new quay, and the only fishing now is for crabs and lobsters.

Walk out to the **main street** and turn left back up to the **car park** to complete the walk. ♦

Dodman Cross

In addition to its Iron Age boundary, Bronze Age barrows and medieval field patterns attest to the Dodman's occupation across millennia. A beacon was established in the 16th century to warn of sea raiders and in 1794 an Admiralty signal station was built to relay shipping information during the Napoleonic War. It was later used by the Coastguard. The prominent granite cross was erected in 1896 as a daymark and warning to passing vessels.

Polruan is a fishing and shipbuilding village sheltered within the Fowey Estuary

walk 9

Polruan & Lantic Bay

Sheltered woodlands and impressive coastal views on this ramble around the Polruan headland

What to expect:
Steep climbs and descents, but otherwise good woodland and coastal paths, some quiet lanes

Distance/Time: 10.5 kilometres/ 6½ miles. Allow 3½ to 4 hours

Start: Lantivet Bay National Trust car park (pay and display)

Grid ref: SX 157 516

Ordnance Survey map: Explorer 107 *St Austell & Liskeard*

Refreshment: The Lugger Inn, Polruan | 01726 870007 | www.theluggerinnpolruan.co.uk OR The Russell Inn, Polruan | 01726 870707 | www.russellinn.co.uk

Walk Outline
Begin by following quiet lanes to Churchtown Farm, passing through the churchyard to descend a wooded combe behind. Emerging onto a lane, the walk climbs to an undulating path across steep, wooded slopes above Pont Pill. Dropping to Polruan harbour, stroll through the village before taking to the cliffs above Wellake and Lantic Bay. Following a strenuous ascent onto the Pencarrow peninsula, the route rises and falls more easily across steep slopes behind Lantivet Bay. A final pull takes the way back across the fields to the car park.

Polruan
Tucked behind the headland within the Fowey estuary, Polruan grew as a prosperous medieval port trading in tin, wine and other goods. Shipbuilding and associated trades developed too and in later years the shipyard specialised in fast vessels to bring fruit from the Mediterranean, Azores and West Indies. The port was used by English privateers during the Hundred Years War and twin blockhouses were built either side of the strait to guard against enemy ships. Polruan's blockhouse is remarkably well preserved today, offering a fine view across the estuary.

Polruan blockhouse

Peacock butterfly

The Walk

1. Go right out of the **car park** and then right again towards **Polruan**. After 800 metres, at a junction, turn off right and follow the narrow lane down to **Churchtown Farm**.

2. Turn into **St Wyllow's churchyard**, where the church is worth exploring. Pass around the eastern end of the building to find a descending path through the **woods** behind emerging onto a lane at the bottom by **cottages**.

3. Climb steeply away to the left, soon leaving through a field gate on the right. Immediately branch left to continue gaining height beside the lane. At a fork higher up, keep right, but shortly after branch left to **Polruan**. Keep going with the main path, which finishes down a long **flight of steps** to meet a narrow street. Walk right down more steps and then left to find the **harbour** at the bottom on the right.

One of Polruan's most colourful characters was Zephania Job, the Smugglers' Banker. Born in St Agnes, he started out as a tin miner, before settling here around 1770 and becoming adept at accounting and the ways of seaborne trade. Job handled the affairs of privateers working from the port both during the American and subsequent French wars. From this, it was only a slight shift to acting as agent for smugglers landing contraband goods from France and the Channel Islands. With many of the county's respected gentry and clergy involved too, he always managed to be a step ahead of the authorities. But Job

Walk 9 – **Polruan** & **Lantic Bay** ♦ 55

Great Lantic Beach seen from the South West Coast Path

was also a successful legitimate merchant and financier as well, providing legal services and even running his own bank. He died at the age of 73, a lifelong bachelor and relatively rich man, with over £7,700 (almost £1m today) going to his nephews and sister once his affairs had been wound up.

4. Climb back and go right along **West Street** to find the **Blockhouse** at its end.

The distinction between privateering and outright piracy was often vague, with letters of marque giving a veneer of legitimacy to roving captains in search of plunder. It

Bird's-eye view of Pont Pill and Polruan from high above Fowey

effectively enabled navies to swell their size or governments to harry their enemies without actually declaring war, while the lucrative reward was a share of the loot or ransom less a kickback going to the government. The English, French, Spanish, Americans and others all employed privateers until the practice was finally brought to an end under the Declaration of Paris in 1859.

Return the way you came, but take the first right up **Battery Lane**. Wind around a left bend and then keep ahead with the **South West Coast Path**. Go left again at the end of the buildings and then right passing a **car park** and a **National Coastwatch Station** to join a street.

5. Carry on past a **school** to a junction and turn right along a drive and into **Furze Park**. The way undulates on across sloping rough meadows towards Pencarrow Head. At a fork beyond **Blackbottle Rock**, keep right to pass behind **Great Lantic Beach**. There follows a steep climb onto the hill. A path leaves through a gate down to the beach, but otherwise keep going uphill, passing through gates higher up. The Coast Path now leads right onto **Pencarrow Head**, passing an outcrop that makes a fine viewpoint.

6. At the tip of the headland, swing left to continue around the coast, undulating above **Watch House Cove**.

Eventually cresting a rise, enter an open field where the path forks at a waypost. Bear left across, making for the leftmost one of two gates in the corner. A hollow path leads out to the lane.

Cross to the gated path opposite, which emerges opposite the **car park**, to complete the walk. ♦

St Wyllow's Church

Wyllow was a 6th-century hermit from Ireland who settled by the River Fowey in Pont. Beheaded for his faith, tradition has it that he then walked to this spot carrying his head and thus a church was established. It is a lovely building and amongst its treasures are medieval bench ends, elaborately carved with shields, foliage and heads, while outside is a 14th-century cross. The novelist Daphne du Maurier was married here in 1932.

Ancient St Michael's Chapel dominates the summit of Rame Head

walk 10

Rame Head

An attractive village, military ruins, an ancient chapel and superb coastal scenery in a 'forgotten' corner of Cornwall

What to expect:
Good paths and tracks, short stretch along lanes

Distance/Time: 10.5 kilometres/ 6½ miles. Allow 3¼ to 4 hours
Start: Cawsand car park (pay and display)
Grid ref: SX 431 502
Ordnance Survey map: Explorer 108 *Lower Tamar Valley & Plymouth*
Refreshment: The Cross Keys Inn | 01752 822706 | www.crosskeysinncawsand.com OR The Old Bakery | 01752 616215 | www.theoldbakery-cawsand.co.uk

Walk Outline

After winding through the town and up past the old fort, the route climbs away across the hillside past Wringford Farm to Wiggle. A quiet lane leads on to the coast, where there is then easy walking across the sloping cliffs to Polhawn. Short, steeper pulls are necessary to reach Rame Head and its ancient chapel. Passing beneath the National Coastwatch Station, the circuit continues along the open coast, eventually turning Penlee Point and then descending gently through woodland back to Cawsand.

Rame Head

Now relatively isolated, this area is often quiet. Yet, over the centuries it has been repeatedly fortified to defend the approaches to Plymouth Sound, the 19th century seeing the greatest proliferation with a new military road, forts and batteries. These and other positions served in two World Wars, but today only the forts at Polhawn and Cawsand remain, now converted into a hotel and housing. The headland is also crowned with a medieval chapel; but even that served as a wartime base for observation and gun positions as well as a radar station.

Ruined chapel, Rame Head

Gannet

The Walk

1. Leaving the bottom of the **car park**, walk down to a **small square** and turn left up **Garrett Street**. Just beyond **The Old Bakery**, look for a **flight of steps** climbing beside **Laleham House**. At the top go briefly right then leave up more steps beside the former **fort**. Cross a drive to yet more steps, and then bear right behind a building on a path leading beneath trees to a field.

2. Head out on a trod, passing through gates at the far end to meet another path. Turn right over a stile and carry on, gently rising across the valley side. Leave at the far side onto a lane.

3. Take the drive opposite to **Wringford Farm**. Through gates, immediately branch off right along a **tree-tunnelled path** that leads into a field. Strike out to the far corner, a path taking the way beyond gently down before swinging beneath trees. Approaching the **old farm house** at **Wiggle**, bear left to emerge onto the bend of a lane. Follow the lane

The 19th-century folly on Penlee Point

left to its end. Reaching a junction, drop right cutting through to the main lane.

4. Cross to the drive opposite, forking off left past an **information board**. Lower down, swing sharp left to continue across the gorse downs of **Wiggle Cliff**. Emerging onto a track go briefly right and then branch off left to bypass a house. Turning up steps to a drive at the entrance to **Polhawn Fort**, cross to more steps opposite and climb to a crossing path. Go right, undulating upwards onto **Rame Head**. Dipping across the narrow neck, climb up to the **hilltop chapel**.

5. Retrace your steps to the neck and now branch right towards Penlee Point. The **Coast Path** remains high, eventually emerging through a gate onto the sharp bend of a track. Keep with the lower branch, ignoring a path shortly forking down to a helipad on the point.

Visible on a clear day is the Eddystone Lighthouse, marking a dangerous shoal 9 miles out. Completed in 1698, the first tower lasted barely five years before being washed away in a storm. The present structure is the fourth, operational since 1882. It is now solar powered and controlled from Harwich.

6. Rounding **Penlee Point**, beneath the site of the **Penlee Battery**, a second path leads off down to a 19th-century **folly** in Gothic style. *Comprising three arched openings, angled to give different views, the grotto was built in 1827 for the visit of the future Queen Adelaide to nearby Mount Edgcumbe.*

Return to the main track, which runs on pleasantly through **woodland**. *In 1859, the threat of French invasion prompted Lord Palmerston, the then Prime Minister, to upgrade the land and seaward defence of the country's naval dockyards. With a budget of over £3m just for Plymouth and Devonport Docks, he established a series of forts, batteries and gun emplacements along the coast to the east and west of The Sound as well as on The Breakwater and Drake's Island. Another line of forts was built to the north between the Plym and the Tamar to defend against land-based attack. But even before they were completed, they had become known as Palmerston's follies; the political climate had shifted and technological advances in artillery design had rendered them obsolete. However, re-armed, many served vital roles during two World Wars and have since been re-furbished while the Penlee Battery is a nature reserve.*

Reaching a fork, bear right, soon joining another track. Follow it left, but then branch off right with the continuing Coast Path. Passing **cottages**, disregard the climbing track and carry on, before long emerging onto a **village street**. Turn down right to the **square** and go left, back to the car park, to complete the walk. ♦

Wildlife on Penlee Point
During spring and summer the sloping cliffs are splashed with the colour of countless wild flowers. Sea pinks, squill, valerian, viper's bugloss and mallow are amongst those to be found, which in turn encourage a profusion of butterflies and other insects. Indeed Penlee is famous for the find of a Green Darner dragonfly in 1998, blown over from America in a storm. Birds seen in the area include ravens, hen harriers, peregrines and short-eared owls.

Useful Information

Visit South Cornwall
South Cornwall's official tourism website covers everything from accommodation and events to attractions and adventure: **www.visitcornwall.com/places/south-cornwall**

Cornwall AONB
www.cornwall-aonb.gov.uk

Selected Tourist Information Centres
The main TICs provide free information on everything from accommodation and transport to what's on and walking advice.

Falmouth	01326 74119 **
Fowey	090 5151 0262 **
Helston	01326 564027
Looe	01503 262072
Mevagissey	01726 842200
Penzance	01736 335530
St Austell	01726 879500
St Just	01736 788165
St Mawes & Roseland	01326 270440
Sennen Cove	01736 871215
Truro	01872 274555

** Charges apply

Rail Travel
Main stations are located at Plymouth/Saltash, St Austell, Truro and Penzance with others serving the coast at Falmouth and Looe: National Rail Enquiries 08457 484950 or **www.nationalrail.com.uk**

Bus Travel
Many places along the South Devon Coast are served by bus: **www.travelinesw.com**

Camping
Devon is a popular area for camping, with many sites owned by or affiliated to the Camping and Caravanning Club: 024 7647 5426 | **www.campingandcaravanningclub.co.uk**